SACRED SPACE

for Advent and the Christmas Season 2013–2014

December 1, 2013, to January 5, 2014

from the website www.sacredspace.ie
Prayer from the Irish Jesuits

ave maria press  notre dame, indiana

acknowledgment

The publisher would like to thank Brian Grogan, S.J., for his kind assistance in making this book possible. Correspondence with the Sacred Space team can be directed to feedback@sacredspace.ie.

Unless otherwise noted, the Scripture quotations contained herein are from the *New Revised Standard Version* Bible, copyright © 1989 by the Division of Christian Education of the National Council of the Churches of Christ in the United States of America. Used by permission. All rights reserved.

Advent retreat by Brian Grogan, S.J., used with permission.

Published under license from Michelle Anderson Publishing Pty Ltd., in Australia.

Founded in 1865, Ave Maria Press is a ministry of the United States Province of Holy Cross.

www.avemariapress.com

Paperback: ISBN-10: 1-59471-436-3, ISBN-13: 978-1-59471-436-8

E-book: ISBN-10: 1-59471-442-8, ISBN-13: 978-1-59471-442-9

Cover design by Andy Wagoner.

Text design by K. Hornyak Bonelli.

Printed and bound in the United States of America.

contents

how to use this booklet

We invite you to make a sacred space in your day and spend ten minutes praying here and now, wherever you are, with the help of a prayer guide and scripture chosen specially for each day of Advent and the Christmas Season. Every place is a sacred space so you may wish to have this book in your desk at work or available to be picked up and read at any time of the day, whilst traveling or on your bedside table, a park bench . . . Remember that God is everywhere, all around us, constantly reaching out to us, even in the most unlikely situations. When we know this, and with a bit of practice, we can pray anywhere.

The following pages will guide you through a session of prayer stages:

Something to think and pray about each day this week
The Presence of God
Freedom
Consciousness
The Word (leads you to the daily scripture and provides help with the text)

Conversation
Conclusion

It is most important to come back to these pages each day of the week, as they are an integral part of each day's prayer and lead to the scripture and inspiration points.

Although written in the first person, the prayers are for "doing" rather than for reading out. Each stage is a kind of exercise or meditation aimed at helping you to get in touch with God and God's presence in your life. We hope that you will join the many people around the world praying with us in our sacred space.

the presence of God

Bless all who worship you, almighty God,
from the rising of the sun to its setting:
from your goodness enrich us,
by your love inspire us,
by your Spirit guide us,
by your power protect us,
in your mercy receive us,
now and always.

december 1–7, 2013

Something to think and pray about each day this week:

The Coming Days

Advent is in many ways the most beautiful and profound time of the Christian year. Advent means "coming," and the season is about our waiting for the most mysterious and wonderful coming of all—into the heart of our lives, our needy lives. The words of St. Paul are relevant: "It is now the moment for you to wake from sleep. For salvation is nearer to us now than when we first became believers; the night is far gone, the day is near. Let us then lay aside the works of darkness and put on the armor of light" (Rom 13:11–12). So over and over, from the heart of the Christian people, and down through the centuries, the prayer has gone up: "Show us, Lord, your steadfast love, and grant us your salvation" and "Come, Lord, and bring us peace. Let us rejoice before you with sincere hearts." We can pray now: "Lord, help us to

wait, with patience, with longing, for your coming—your coming into our poor lives. As once
your people waited, and you came in our midst as
a child to be among us—so help us now to wait,
hope, and love what we wait for: your coming,
and your peace."

The Presence of God
Lord, help me to be fully alive to your holy
presence.
Enfold me in your love.
Let my heart become one with yours.

Freedom
Many countries are at this moment suffering the
agonies of war.
I bow my head in thanksgiving for my freedom.
I pray for all prisoners and captives.

Consciousness
At this moment, Lord, I turn my thoughts to you.
I will leave aside my chores and preoccupations.
I will take rest and refreshment in your presence
Lord.

The Word

The Word of God comes down to us through the scriptures.

May the Holy Spirit enlighten my mind and my heart to respond to the gospel teachings.

(Please turn to your scripture on the following pages. Inspiration points are there should you need them. When you are ready, return here to continue.)

Conversation

Sometimes I wonder what I might say if I were to meet you in person, Lord.

I might say "Thank You, Lord" for always being there for me.

I know with certainty there were times when you carried me.

When through your strength I got through the dark times in my life.

Conclusion

Glory be to the Father, and to the Son, and to the Holy Spirit,

As it was in the beginning, is now and ever shall be, World without end. Amen.

Sunday 1st December,
First Sunday of Advent   Matthew 24:37–44

For as the days of Noah were, so will be the coming of the Son of Man. For as in those days before the flood they were eating and drinking, marrying and giving in marriage, until the day Noah entered the ark, and they knew nothing until the flood came and swept them all away, so too will be the coming of the Son of Man. Then two will be in the field; one will be taken and one will be left. Two women will be grinding meal together; one will be taken and one will be left. Keep awake therefore, for you do not know on what day your Lord is coming. But understand this: if the owner of the house had known in what part of the night the thief was coming, he would have stayed awake and would not have let his house be broken into. Therefore you also must be ready, for the Son of Man is coming at an unexpected hour.

- Jesus is not asking us to stay awake all night, but to live in the present, so that I can recognize the Lord when he appears in my life. He shows himself in the unrehearsed moments, the interruptions and accidents that can throw me off balance.

• Teach me, Lord, to recognize you wherever I encounter you.

Monday 2nd December   Matthew 8:5–11

When Jesus entered Capernaum, a centurion came to him, appealing to him and saying, "Lord, my servant is lying at home paralyzed, in terrible distress." And he said to him, "I will come and cure him." The centurion answered, "Lord, I am not worthy to have you come under my roof; but only speak the word, and my servant will be healed. For I also am a man under authority, with soldiers under me; and I say to one, 'Go,' and he goes, and to another, 'Come,' and he comes, and to my slave, 'Do this,' and the slave does it." When Jesus heard him, he was amazed and said to those who followed him, "Truly I tell you, in no one in Israel have I found such faith. I tell you, many will come from east and west and will eat with Abraham and Isaac and Jacob in the kingdom of heaven."

• It was not easy for an officer in the imperial army to come as a beggar to an itinerant Jewish rabbi. The centurion made an extraordinary leap out of his own culture and pride into a recognition of Jesus' power. Jesus was amazed at his faith.

- Have I the insight to perceive holiness and God's hand at work around me, or am I imprisoned by the stereotypes of my culture?

Tuesday 3rd December,
St. Francis Xavier   Matthew 28:16–20

Now the eleven disciples went to Galilee, to the mountain to which Jesus had directed them. When they saw him, they worshipped him; but some doubted. And Jesus came and said to them, "All authority in heaven and on earth has been given to me. Go therefore and make disciples of all nations, baptizing them in the name of the Father and of the Son and of the Holy Spirit, and teaching them to obey everything that I have commanded you. And remember, I am with you always, to the end of the age."

- "They worshipped him; but some doubted." When I intend to praise God, to pray, I may also find doubt presses in on me. Can I include those doubts in my prayer?

- Can I hear the Lord saying to me, "Remember, I am with you always"?

Wednesday 4th December   Matthew 15:29–37

After Jesus had left that place, he passed along the Sea of Galilee, and he went up the mountain, where he sat down. Great crowds came to him, bringing with them the lame, the maimed, the blind, the mute, and many others. They put them at his feet, and he cured them, so that the crowd was amazed when they saw the mute speaking, the maimed whole, the lame walking, and the blind seeing. And they praised the God of Israel. Then Jesus called his disciples to him and said, "I have compassion for the crowd, because they have been with me now for three days and have nothing to eat; and I do not want to send them away hungry, for they might faint on the way." The disciples said to him, "Where are we to get enough bread in the desert to feed so great a crowd?" Jesus asked them, "How many loaves have you?" They said, "Seven, and a few small fish." Then ordering the crowd to sit down on the ground, he took the seven loaves and the fish; and after giving thanks he broke them and gave them to the disciples, and the disciples gave them to the crowds. And all of them ate and were filled; and they took up the broken pieces left over, seven baskets full.

- Jesus had compassion for the crowds. He sees me among them and knows my needs. I tell him where I am most challenged and listen for his word.

- Fullness of life and ability were offered to the sick and to those in need. Jesus calls me to full life, forgiving and healing any lack of capacity or effort that I have, inviting me to be a fuller sign of God's presence.

Thursday 5th December   Matthew 7:21, 24–27

Jesus said to the people, "Not everyone who says to me, 'Lord, Lord,' will enter the kingdom of heaven, but only one who does the will of my Father in heaven. . . . Everyone then who hears these words of mine and acts on them will be like a wise man who built his house on rock. The rain fell, the floods came, and the winds blew and beat on that house, but it did not fall, because it had been founded on rock. And everyone who hears these words of mine and does not act on them will be like a foolish man who built his house on sand. The rain fell, and the floods came, and the winds blew and beat against that house, and it fell—and great was its fall!"

- Hearing or reading the Word is important, but is not the end. I take time to let the Word of God settle into the shape of my life. I take care not to let it merely stay in my mind, but to let it touch my heart and desires.

- I ask God to help me be present to the Word. I ask for sincerity and integrity, and that my words may not just remain sounds but are also backed up by my way of living.

Friday 6th December   Matthew 9:27–31

As Jesus went on his way, two blind men followed him, crying loudly, "Have mercy on us, Son of David!" When he entered the house, the blind men came to him; and Jesus said to them, "Do you believe that I am able to do this?" They said to him, "Yes, Lord." Then he touched their eyes and said, "According to your faith let it be done to you." And their eyes were opened. Then Jesus sternly ordered them, "See that no one knows of this." But they went away and spread the news about him throughout that district.

- The blind men remind me of the need to be persistent in my prayer. Is what I ask God for now in my mind during the day? Do I look with expectation and hope to see how God is answering me? If I don't, what might my lack of perseverance say?

- I give thanks to God for those times when my eyes have been opened, and I ask him to lead me to appreciate truth.

Saturday 7th December
Matthew 9:35–10:1, 6–8

Jesus went about all the cities and villages, teaching in their synagogues, and proclaiming the good news of the kingdom, and curing every disease and every sickness. When he saw the crowds, he had compassion for them, because they were harassed and helpless, like sheep without a shepherd. Then he said to his disciples, "The harvest is plentiful, but the laborers are few; therefore ask the Lord of the harvest to send out laborers into his harvest." Then Jesus summoned his twelve disciples and gave them authority over unclean spirits, to cast them out, and to cure every disease and every sickness. These twelve Jesus sent out with the following instructions: "Go rather to the lost sheep of the house of Israel. As you go, proclaim the good news, 'The kingdom of heaven has come near.' Cure the sick, raise the dead, cleanse the lepers, cast out demons. You received without payment; give without payment."

- In Jesus' time, people believed that those who had serious psychiatric illnesses were "possessed" by demons. Even today we talk of alcoholics as being possessed by the "demon" drink. Maybe I need to examine my "demons."

- Jesus' good news was the love and forgiveness of God poured out on all of us, whatever our "demons." When we love and forgive others, especially the poor and those on the margins, we spread the good news of God's kingdom, God's reign of love.

The Second Week of Advent
december 8–14

Something to think and pray about each day this week:

The Waiting Days

Waiting takes up a large part of our lives. Often we see waiting as "nonproductive," as a waste of time, and are frustrated. But waiting, and indeed the helplessness of it, can be more meaningful and fruitful than all the achieving we feel will give us status and fulfillment. A mother awaits the birth of her child. I wait for the homecoming of someone I cherish and love. I wait, when all human efforts run out, for what is right and just. Advent shows how beautiful waiting is. Years ago W. H. Vanstone wrote *The Stature of Waiting*, on the meaning and fruitfulness of waiting. And much further back John Henry Newman preached one of his most evocative Oxford sermons for Advent, titled "Watching," on how we as Christians are called in all things to "look out" for Christ, to "watch" and be alert for his coming, in the midst of our daily lives, as well as at the end. Our prayer especially can have that element to it, of "being on the watch" as Jesus puts it in the Gospel. Lord, let me be prayerful, and watchful, this Advent.

The Presence of God
God is with me, but more,
God is within me, giving me existence.
Let me dwell for a moment on God's life-giving presence
in my body, my mind, my heart, and in the whole of my life.

Freedom
God is not foreign to my freedom.
Instead the Spirit breathes life into my most intimate desires,
gently nudging me towards all that is good.
I ask for the grace to let myself be enfolded by the Spirit.

Consciousness
Help me, Lord, to be more conscious of your presence.
Teach me to recognize your presence in others.
Fill my heart with gratitude for the times your love has been shown to me through the care of others.

The Word

I read the Word of God slowly, a few times
over, and I listen to what God is saying to me.
(Please turn to your scripture on the following
pages. Inspiration points are there should you
need them. When you are ready, return here to
continue.)

Conversation

How has God's Word moved me?
Has it left me cold?
Has it consoled me or moved me to act in a new
way?
I imagine Jesus standing or sitting beside me,
I turn and share my feelings with him.

Conclusion

Glory be to the Father, and to the Son,
and to the Holy Spirit,
As it was in the beginning, is now and ever shall be,
World without end. Amen.

Sunday 8th December,
Second Sunday of Advent Matthew 3:1–6

In those days John the Baptist appeared in the wilderness of Judea, proclaiming, "Repent, for the kingdom of heaven has come near." This is the one of whom the prophet Isaiah spoke when he said, "The voice of one crying out in the wilderness: 'Prepare the way of the Lord, make his paths straight.'" Now John wore clothing of camel's hair with a leather belt around his waist, and his food was locusts and wild honey. Then the people of Jerusalem and all Judea were going out to him, and all the region along the Jordan, and they were baptized by him in the river Jordan, confessing their sins.

- Isn't it extraordinary how a mortified man draws people. We admire one whose needs are minimal, who is the master of his own appetites, who has a deep interior freedom. John the Baptist, with minimal clothes and minimal food, was a magnet. People trusted him because clearly he could not be bought.

- Where are the chains on me, the appetites which I have not mastered, and that pull me in ways I do not want? Help me towards a freer heart and body, Lord.

Monday 9th December, The Immaculate Conception of the Blessed Virgin Mary — Luke 1:30–33

The angel said to her, "Do not be afraid, Mary, for you have found favor with God. And now, you will conceive in your womb and bear a son, and you will name him Jesus. He will be great, and will be called the Son of the Most High, and the Lord God will give to him the throne of his ancestor David. He will reign over the house of Jacob forever, and of his kingdom there will be no end."

- We know this encounter between God's messenger and Mary changed the world. Whatever hopes she held for her life, she let go of in this moment and embraced God's plan.

- Can we look beyond this momentous event to delve into our own responses? Can we let go of own individual fears, and even our plans, to embrace hope? Can we say, "I don't know what this all means, but I trust that good things will happen"?

Tuesday 10th December   Isaiah 40:3–5

A voice cries out: "In the wilderness prepare the way of the Lord, make straight in the desert a highway for our God. Every valley shall be lifted up, and every mountain and hill be made low; the uneven ground shall become level, and the rough places a plain. Then the glory of the Lord shall be revealed, and all people shall see it together, for the mouth of the Lord has spoken."

- "Prepare the way of the Lord." This is the essence of this season of Advent. As Isaiah sees it, the earth-shaking preparations of the revealing of the glory of God are themselves the gift of God.

- Can I apply this to myself and my own preparations to meet the Lord? Do the obstacles between me and new life—small or great—seem very immovable, beyond my efforts?

Wednesday 11th December   Matthew 11:28–30

J esus said, "Come to me, all you that are weary and are carrying heavy burdens, and I will give you rest. Take my yoke upon you, and learn from me; for I am gentle and humble in heart, and you will find rest for your souls. For my yoke is easy, and my burden is light."

- For many people Christmas is a time of stress—dealing with concerns about costs, food preparations, or long-standing family compromises and conflicts.

- Lord, open our hearts to your love, to know the security and depth of belonging, to recognize how we all belong in Jesus the Christ.

Thursday 12th December   Matthew 11:11–15

Jesus said to the crowds, "Truly I tell you, among those born of women no one has arisen greater than John the Baptist; yet the least in the kingdom of heaven is greater than he. From the days of John the Baptist until now the kingdom of heaven has suffered violence, and the violent take it by force. For all the prophets and the law prophesied until John came; and if you are willing to accept it, he is Elijah who is to come. Let anyone with ears listen!"

- John may be the greatest figure of the past, but from Jesus' perspective—now that the Messiah has appeared—whoever believes in Jesus and accepts his teaching about God's kingdom is greater than John. But Jesus remains entwined with John the Baptist, as he does with Elijah, as well as with the apostles and the women who follow him.

- In the same way, we are entwined with Jesus and with all those who are part of the journey with Jesus to God.

Friday 13th December   Matthew 11:16–19

Jesus spoke to the crowds, "But to what will I compare this generation? It is like children sitting in the marketplaces and calling to one another, 'We played the flute for you, and you did not dance; we wailed, and you did not mourn.' For John came neither eating nor drinking, and they say, 'He has a demon'; the Son of Man came eating and drinking, and they say, 'Look, a glutton and a drunkard, a friend of tax collectors and sinners!' Yet wisdom is vindicated by her deeds."

- Jesus illustrates two negative responses to the ministries of both himself and of John the Baptist: John is too severe for them; he "has a demon." Jesus is too lax; he is "a friend of tax collectors and sinners."

- Jesus' ministry may disturb us because he preaches a God of compassion, which may not be what we expect. How do we try to make God "fit in" with what we want?

Saturday 14th December   Matthew 17:10–13

And the disciples asked him, "Why, then, do the scribes say that Elijah must come first?" He replied, "Elijah is indeed coming and will restore all things; but I tell you that Elijah has already come, and they did not recognize him, but they did to him whatever they pleased. So also the Son of Man is about to suffer at their hands." Then the disciples understood that he was speaking to them about John the Baptist.

- The Jews expected Elijah to come as a great and terrible reformer, making the world perfect before the Messiah would arrive. Jesus insists that God works not through a powerful cleansing fire, but through sacrificial love.

- Jesus was always aware that he was to suffer; the crib is most realistic when the cross is in the background, close by. Lord, teach me to follow you, to accept this challenge, to understand love and suffering.

december 15–21

Something to think and pray about each day this week:

Becoming a Little One

In the Bible, it was the poor who were especially conscious of God's working in their lives. Called the *anawim* in Hebrew, they were often just a remnant, a small number, "a people humble and lowly" (Zep 3:12), who took refuge in God alone. In the Gospel of Luke, people like Elizabeth and Zechariah, John the Baptist, Simeon and Anna, and above all Joseph and Mary, are portrayed as belonging to the *anawim*. They are not the great people walking the earth but the hidden ones, living with faith, with humanity, and in truth. It is to them God comes, and especially to Mary. Mary, in response to the Angel, says in effect: "Let what God wants come about in my life" (cf. Lk 1:38). And Elizabeth would then say to her cousin: "Yes, blessed is she who believed that the promise made her by the Lord would be fulfilled" (cf. Lk 1:45). Lord, help me in the poverty of my heart to be open to you—to your coming, your love, blessing, and peace. Help me to depend on you, for you are Lord of my heart, my deepest peace, and the surest guide along the path of my life. Lord, place me among the *anawim*, to be blessed by you through the gift of believing.

The Presence of God

What is present to me is what has a hold on my becoming.
I reflect on the presence of God always there in love,
amidst the many things that have a hold on me.
I pause and pray that I may let God affect my becoming in this precise moment.

Freedom

There are very few people who realize what God would make of them if they abandoned themselves into his hands,
and let themselves be formed by his grace. (St. Ignatius)
I ask for the grace to trust myself totally to God's love.

Consciousness

In the presence of my loving Creator,

I look honestly at my feelings over the last day,
the highs, the lows, and the level ground.
Can I see where the Lord has been present?

The Word

God speaks to each one of us individually. I need
to listen to hear what he is saying to me. Read
the text a few times, then listen. (Please turn to
your scripture on the following pages. Inspiration points are there should you need them.
When you are ready, return here to continue.)

Conversation

What is stirring in me as I pray?
Am I consoled, troubled, left cold?
I imagine Jesus himself standing or sitting at my
side,
and share my feelings with him.

Conclusion

Glory be to the Father, and to the Son,
and to the Holy Spirit,
As it was in the beginning, is now and ever shall
be,
World without end. Amen.

Sunday 15th December,
Third Sunday of Advent   Matthew 11:2–11

When John heard in prison what the Messiah was doing, he sent word by his disciples and said to him, "Are you the one who is to come, or are we to wait for another?" Jesus answered them, "Go and tell John what you hear and see: the blind receive their sight, the lame walk, the lepers are cleansed, the deaf hear, the dead are raised, and the poor have good news brought to them. And blessed is anyone who takes no offense at me." As they went away, Jesus began to speak to the crowds about John: "What did you go out into the wilderness to look at? A reed shaken by the wind? What then did you go out to see? Someone dressed in soft robes? Look, those who wear soft robes are in royal palaces. What then did you go out to see? A prophet? Yes, I tell you, and more than a prophet. This is the one about whom it is written, 'See, I am sending my messenger ahead of you, who will prepare your way before you.' Truly I tell you, among those born of women no one has arisen greater than John the Baptist; yet the least in the kingdom of heaven is greater than he."

- There is real comfort in this story. John the Baptist had his moments of darkness. Imprisoned in Herod's dungeon, he wondered, "Am I a fool? Was I wrong about Jesus?" He does not just brood on the question but sends messengers to Jesus. And Jesus does not send back reassurances; he just asks the messengers to open their eyes and see the evidence of Jesus' life.

- Lord, in my moments of doubt and darkness, may I fill my eyes with you.

Monday 16th December   Matthew 21:23–27

When Jesus entered the temple, the chief priests and the elders of the people came to him as he was teaching, and said, "By what authority are you doing these things, and who gave you this authority?" Jesus said to them, "I will also ask you one question; if you tell me the answer, then I will also tell you by what authority I do these things. Did the baptism of John come from heaven, or was it of human origin?" And they argued with one another, "If we say, 'From heaven,' he will say to us, 'Why then did you not believe him?' But if we say, 'Of human origin,' we are afraid of the crowd; for all regard John as a prophet." So they answered Jesus, "We do not know." And he said to them, "Neither will I tell you by what authority I am doing these things."

- Jesus does not engage in futile discussion. There are times when words may get in the way, when no amount of speech will help.

- Am I sometimes like the priests and elders? Quizzing, figuring out, arguing, debating? Jesus values a faith that is lively, engaged, generous, and uncomplicated. I spend time with Jesus, careful not to be always talking and quizzing.

Tuesday 17th December   Genesis 49:1–2, 8–10

Jacob called his sons, and said to them, "Assemble and hear, O sons of Jacob; listen to Israel your father. Judah, your brothers shall praise you; your hand shall be on the neck of your enemies; your father's sons shall bow down before you. Judah is a lion's whelp; from the prey, my son, you have gone up. He crouches down, he stretches out like a lion, like a lioness—who dares rouse him up? The scepter shall not depart from Judah, nor the ruler's staff from between his feet, until tribute comes to him; and the obedience of the peoples is his."

- "The scepter shall not pass from Judah until . . . the obedience of the peoples is his." In the words of the old man, we Christians hear the promise of the one who is to come.

- Can I begin to let myself feel some of the hope and expectation of those who wait for a promised Messiah?

Wednesday 18th December   Matthew 1:18–25

Now the birth of Jesus the Messiah took place in this way. When his mother Mary had been engaged to Joseph, but before they lived together, she was found to be with child from the Holy Spirit. Her husband Joseph, being a righteous man and unwilling to expose her to public disgrace, planned to dismiss her quietly. But just when he had resolved to do this, an angel of the Lord appeared to him in a dream and said, "Joseph, son of David, do not be afraid to take Mary as your wife, for the child conceived in her is from the Holy Spirit. She will bear a son, and you are to name him Jesus, for he will save his people from their sins." All this took place to fulfill what had been spoken by the Lord through the prophet: "Look, the virgin shall conceive and bear a son, and they shall name him Emmanuel," which means, "God is with us." When Joseph awoke from sleep, he did as the angel of the Lord commanded him; he took her as his wife, but had no marital relations with her until she had borne a son; and he named him Jesus.

- Joseph often seems to be in the shadows of the nativity scene. I spend some time with him today, appreciating his integrity, valuing his ability to discern, and recognizing that God gave him a message of encouragement.

- Joseph, although he had made up his mind, was prepared to let his dream speak. I ask for the grace to be able to bring my decisions before God, allowing my heart to be shaped and my mind to be changed.

Thursday 19th December
Psalm 70 (71):3–6, 16–17

Be to me a rock of refuge, a strong fortress, to save me, for you are my rock and my fortress. Rescue me, O my God, from the hand of the wicked, from the grasp of the unjust and cruel. For you, O Lord, are my hope, my trust, O Lord, from my youth. Upon you I have leaned from my birth;

it was you who took me from my mother's womb. I will come praising the mighty deeds of the Lord God, I will praise your righteousness, yours alone. O God, from my youth you have taught me, and I still proclaim your wondrous deeds.

- The Psalms express this most fundamental hope; that our refuge, our rest, and security lie in God alone.

- Lord, teach us to speak with the clear voice of the psalmist, to acknowledge that God is with each of us from the moment of our birth—today, yesterday, and tomorrow.

Friday 20th December   Luke 1:26–29

In the sixth month the angel Gabriel was sent by God to a town in Galilee called Nazareth, to a virgin whose name was Mary. And he came to her and said, "Greetings, favored one! The Lord is with you." But she was much perplexed by his words and pondered what sort of greeting this might be.

- "The Lord is with you." This encounter between God's messenger and Mary is full of mystery. In her response, Mary shows us how to pray and how to seek the will of God in our daily encounters.

- As the end of the Advent season brings the promise of God's incarnate Son, Jesus, what can we learn from Mary's response?

Saturday 21st December   Luke 1:39–45

In those days Mary set out and went with haste to a Judean town in the hill country, where she entered the house of Zechariah and greeted Elizabeth. When Elizabeth heard Mary's greeting, the child leapt in her womb. And Elizabeth was filled with the Holy Spirit and exclaimed with a loud cry, "Blessed are you among women, and blessed is the fruit of your womb. And why has this happened to me, that the mother of my Lord comes to me? For as soon as I heard the sound of your greeting, the child in my womb leapt for joy. And blessed is she who believed that there would be a fulfillment of what was spoken to her by the Lord."

- Mary has just learned that she is to be the mother of God. She does not bask in being the celebrity of all celebrities but rather puts on sandals and cloak and walks to Judea to help her pregnant cousin.

- Think of occasions when I served and took joy in it; not as a paid job but as a labor of love, and the delight that comes from thinking more about others than about myself. St. Paul quotes Jesus as saying, "It is more blessed to give than to receive" (Acts 20:35).

december 22–28

Something to think and pray about each day this week:

Wait No More

Coming closer to Christmas, there is naturally a greater focus in Christian prayer and liturgy on the historical waiting of Mary, and of her people, for the promised Messiah. Above all, Mary's waiting, in her pregnancy, can be mingled with ours this Advent. For Mary is not far away, but close. Her expectation, her prayer, is joined with ours. Deep from the heart of history, a great prayer arises and joins with ours too. For from the eighth century, the great "O Antiphon" prayers ring out for us now in the Christian liturgy. "O Wisdom," "O Adonai and leader of Israel," "O stock of Jesse," "O key of David," "O Rising Sun," "O King whom all the nations desire," and finally "O Emmanuel." "O come!" Come and save us, free all those in darkness, and do not delay. Our prayer now, our deep hunger, is joined to that crying from the heart of history—and therefore too from the depths of a needy world today. And it all rises to the living God, who is truly coming to us, in the little Child to be born of Mary.

The Presence of God
God is with me, but more, God is within me.
Let me dwell for a moment on God's life-giving presence
in my body, in my mind, in my heart,
as I sit here, right now.

Freedom
A thick and shapeless tree-trunk would never believe
that it could become a statue, admired as a miracle of sculpture,
and would never submit itself to the chisel of the sculptor,
who sees by her genius what she can make of it.
(St. Ignatius)
I ask for the grace to let myself be shaped by my loving Creator.

Consciousness
Knowing that God loves me unconditionally,
I can afford to be honest about how I am.

How has the last day been, and how do I feel now?
I share my feelings openly with the Lord.

The Word
I read the Word of God slowly, a few times over, and I listen to what God is saying to me. (Please turn to your scripture on the following pages. Inspiration points are there should you need them. When you are ready, return here to continue.)

Conversation
Do I notice myself reacting as I pray with the Word of God?
Do I feel challenged, comforted, angry?
Imagining Jesus sitting or standing by me, I speak out my feelings,
as one trusted friend to another.

Conclusion
Glory be to the Father, and to the Son, and to the Holy Spirit,
As it was in the beginning, is now and ever shall be,
World without end. Amen.

Sunday 22nd December,
Fourth Sunday of Advent   Romans 1:1–7

Paul, a servant of Jesus Christ, called to be an apostle, set apart for the gospel of God, which he promised beforehand through his prophets in the holy scriptures, the gospel concerning his Son, who was descended from David according to the flesh and was declared to be Son of God with power according to the spirit of holiness by resurrection from the dead, Jesus Christ our Lord, through whom we have received grace and apostleship to bring about the obedience of faith among all the Gentiles for the sake of his name, including yourselves who are called to belong to Jesus Christ, to all God's beloved in Rome, who are called to be saints: Grace to you and peace from God our Father and the Lord Jesus Christ.

- As Paul presents himself to the believers in Rome, he echoes the nativity stories we read in both Luke and Matthew: the child Jesus is "son of David," sprung from the Jewish tradition, and Jesus is also "son of God," through the power of his resurrection. This Jesus brings salvation to the Jews and to Gentiles alike.

What is my Christian ministry? How would I describe myself? What are the key points in my Christian journey?

Monday 23rd December   Luke 1:57–66

Now the time came for Elizabeth to give birth, and she bore a son. Her neighbors and relatives heard that the Lord had shown his great mercy to her, and they rejoiced with her. On the eighth day they came to circumcise the child, and they were going to name him Zechariah after his father. But his mother said, "No; he is to be called John." They said to her, "None of your relatives has this name." Then they began motioning to his father to find out what name he wanted to give him. He asked for a writing tablet and wrote, "His name is John." And all of them were amazed. Immediately his mouth was opened and his tongue freed, and he began to speak, praising God. Fear came over all their neighbors, and all these things were talked about throughout the entire hill country of Judea. All who heard them pondered them and said, "What then will this child become?" For, indeed, the hand of the Lord was with him.

- Even in his old age, Zechariah was ready to break from the old patterns. I ask for the help that I need to step away from usual patterns and to follow God's call.

- I pray for all children: may the joy and hope that they experience live and grow into a deep appreciation of God's goodness.

Tuesday 24th December   Luke 1:67–79

Then his father Zechariah was filled with the Holy Spirit and spoke this prophecy: "Blessed be the Lord God of Israel, for he has looked favorably on his people and redeemed them. He has raised up a mighty savior for us in the house of his servant David, as he spoke through the mouth of his holy prophets from of old, that we would be saved from our enemies and from the hand of all who hate us. Thus he has shown the mercy promised to our ancestors, and has remembered his holy covenant, the oath that he swore to our ancestor Abraham, to grant us that we, being rescued from the hands of our enemies, might serve him without fear, in holiness and righteousness before him all our days. And you, child, will be called the prophet of the Most High; for you will go before the Lord to prepare his ways, to give knowledge of salvation to his people by the forgiveness of their sins. By the tender mercy of our God, the dawn from on high will break upon us, to give light to those who sit in darkness and in the shadow of death, to guide our feet into the way of peace."

- Allow this psalm of thanks and praise to be made for you, your Benedictus. Zechariah made this prayer for his son, John. It was a prayer grown and made in love. We are now the ones who go before the Lord; our love and care can be the dawn breaking into the lives of others, giving light to all in darkness.

- Take what is suitable from this great prayer, said each morning throughout the church, and let it link you with the living Christ.

Wednesday 25th December,
Feast of the Nativity of the Lord   John 1:1–5

In the beginning was the Word, and the Word was with God, and the Word was God. He was in the beginning with God. All things came into being through him, and without him not one thing came into being. What has come into being in him was life, and the life was the light of all people. The light shines in the darkness, and the darkness did not overcome it.

- The Word lives among us. I let this truth sink in more deeply, giving time to allow joy and gratitude to be my response to God's act of faith in me.

- Among all the lights of this Christmas, I cherish the light that prayer brings to me. I am reassured by the assertion that darkness does not overcome the light, and pray that all who celebrate this feast may experience light and joy.

Thursday 26th December,
St. Stephen, the first martyr
Matthew 10:17–22

Jesus said to his apostles, "Beware of them, for they will hand you over to councils and flog you in their synagogues; and you will be dragged before governors and kings because of me, as a testimony to them and the Gentiles. When they hand you over, do not worry about how you are to speak or what you are to say; for what you are to say will be given to you at that time; for it is not you who speak, but the Spirit of your Father speaking through you. Brother will betray brother to death, and a father his child, and children will rise against parents and have them put to death;

and you will be hated by all because of my name. But the one who endures to the end will be saved."

- St. Stephen, in the midst of his sufferings, placed his trust in God. Jesus' words may well have echoed in his ears: "When they hand you over, do not worry about how you are to speak or what you are to say. You will be given at that moment what you are to say."

- Wisdom, it is said, is making peace with the unchangeable. Do I make peace with any suffering that comes my way?

Friday 27th December, St. John, Evangelist
John 20:1–8

Early on the first day of the week, while it was still dark, Mary Magdalene came to the tomb and saw that the stone had been removed from the tomb. So she ran and went to Simon Peter and the other disciple, the one whom Jesus loved, and said to them, "They have taken the Lord out of the tomb, and we do not know where they have laid him." Then Peter and the other disciple set out and went toward the tomb. The two were running together, but the other disciple outran Peter and reached the tomb first. He bent down to look in and saw the linen wrappings lying there, but he did not go in. Then Simon Peter came, following him, and went into the tomb. He saw the linen wrappings lying there, and the cloth that had been on Jesus' head, not lying with the linen wrappings but rolled up in a place by itself. Then the other disciple, who reached the tomb first, also went in, and he saw and believed.

- The memory of St. John links the end of Jesus' passion and death with the new life of the resurrection; it links Christmas with Easter. We know by faith that the Christ child is the risen Lord. Christmas is the feast of glory, the glory of God hidden in the child who would rise from death.

- The glory of God is hidden in each of God's people. In prayer we can allow our faith in the mystery of the risen Emmanuel to grow and to reach out to embrace all, so that we see the incarnate and risen God in each person we meet.

Saturday 28th December, The Holy Innocents   Matthew 2:16–18

When Herod saw that he had been tricked by the wise men, he was infuriated, and he sent and killed all the children in and around

Bethlehem who were two years old or under, according to the time that he had learned from the wise men. Then was fulfilled what had been spoken through the prophet Jeremiah: "A voice was heard in Ramah, wailing and loud lamentation, Rachel weeping for her children; she refused to be consoled, because they are no more."

- Matthew uses Old Testament parallels to show how salvation history unfolds. Just as Joseph, of multi-coloured dream-coat fame, interprets dreams, so does Joseph, Mary's husband. Pharaoh tried to slay all the male children of the Hebrews, only to have one of them, Moses, escape and become the savior of his people. The tyrant Herod, not wanting any rivals, orders the massacre of all male children two years and under in Bethlehem and its vicinity. But Jesus escapes and he, in his turn, becomes the new savior of his people.

- While we don't know the number of children killed, there would certainly have been "sobbing and lamentation" by the children's parents. We pray for all parents who know the pain of burying a child.

december 29, 2013–january 5, 2014

Something to think and pray about each day this week:

Building from Nothing

If Jesus were to appear in our world, he would be born unnoticed, to a good, struggling family in Ecuador, Uzbekistan, or some place usually out of the news. People would be puzzled, "Where is that place?" He would not be on television, nor would he occupy a center of power or wealth. He would be pushed around, slandered and criticized. He would speak simple truths and some would listen to him and recognize the voice of God. The good news would spread slowly, as it did two thousand years ago. It would graft onto whatever was good in the world. The brokers of power and wealth would not notice it, nor offer it their sponsorship. The happy irony of today is that after the first two thousand years, the good news is so widespread that, whether they know it or not, the whole human race is richer for Jesus' birthday.

The Presence of God
As I sit here, the beating of my heart,
the ebb and flow of my breathing, the move-
ments of my mind
are all signs of God's ongoing creation of me.
I pause for a moment, and become aware of this
presence of God within me.

Freedom
I ask for the grace to let go of my own concerns
and be open to what God is asking of me,
to let myself be guided and formed by my loving
Creator.

Consciousness
In the presence of my loving Creator,
I look honestly at my feelings over the last day,
the highs, the lows, and the level ground.
Can I see where the Lord has been present?

The Word
I take my time to read the Word of God, slowly,
a few times, allowing myself to dwell on anything that strikes me. (Please turn to your scripture on the following pages. Inspiration points
are there should you need them. When you are
ready, return here to continue.)

Conversation

Remembering that I am still in God's presence,
I imagine Jesus himself standing or sitting beside
me,
and say whatever is on my mind, whatever is in
my heart,
speaking as one friend to another.

Conclusion

Glory be to the Father, and to the Son,
and to the Holy Spirit,
As it was in the beginning, is now and ever shall
be,
World without end. Amen.

Sunday 29th December,
The Holy Family   Matthew 2:13–15, 19–23

Now after they had left, an angel of the Lord appeared to Joseph in a dream and said, "Get up, take the child and his mother, and flee to Egypt, and remain there until I tell you; for Herod is about to search for the child, to destroy him." Then Joseph got up, took the child and his mother by night, and went to Egypt, and remained there until the death of Herod. This was to fulfill what had been spoken by the Lord through the prophet, "Out of Egypt I have called my son." When Herod died, an angel of the Lord suddenly appeared in a dream to Joseph in Egypt and said, "Get up, take the child and his mother, and go to the land of Israel, for those who were seeking the child's life are dead." Then Joseph got up, took the child and his mother, and went to the land of Israel. But when he heard that Archelaus was ruling over Judea in place of his father Herod, he was afraid to go there. And after being warned in a dream, he went away to the district of Galilee. There he made his home in a town called Nazareth, so that what had been spoken through the prophets might be fulfilled, "He will be called a Nazorean."

- Why choose this story to celebrate the Holy Family? It is not a story of peace, but rather of drama, hazards and difficult decisions. Jesus and his family are displaced persons seeking a place to live.

- Lord, you have tasted human uncertainties, and the difficulties of survival. Your mother, so blissfully happy when she prayed the *Magnificat*, had to adjust rapidly to homelessness and the life of asylum-seekers. Let me be equally adaptable when you ask me to taste uncertainties and plans going awry.

Monday 30th December   Luke 2:36–40

There was also a prophet, Anna the daughter of Phanuel, of the tribe of Asher. She was of a great age, having lived with her husband for seven years after her marriage, then as a widow to the age of eighty-four. She never left the temple but worshipped there with fasting and prayer night and day. At that moment she came, and began to praise God and to speak about the child to all who were looking for the redemption of Jerusalem. When they had finished everything required by the law of the Lord, they returned to Galilee, to their own town of Nazareth. The child grew and became strong, filled with wisdom; and the favor of God was upon him.

- Mary, Joseph, and their baby return to their hometown of Nazareth, and Luke tells us, "the child grew and became strong, filled with wisdom." In order to be the model for his disciples, Jesus had to be fully human. Jesus learned step-by-step, as every human must: how to lace his sandals, how to react to skinned knees, and what it meant to be Jesus of Nazareth and Son of God.

- What does all this tell me about my image of Jesus?

Tuesday 31st December   **John 1:16–18**

From his fullness we have all received, grace upon grace. The law indeed was given through Moses; grace and truth came through Jesus Christ. No one has ever seen God. It is God the only Son, who is close to the Father's heart, who has made him known.

- Taking time to pray provides me with a way to receive the truth and grace that God wants to offer me. I prepare myself to receive blessings from the very heart of God.

- "Grace upon grace"; I picture an abundance of blessing, a cascade of goodness. This is what God desires for me. I ask that I not be content with less.

Wednesday 1st January, Solemnity of Mary, Mother of God

Luke 2:16–21

So they went with haste and found Mary and Joseph, and the child lying in the manger. When they saw this, they made known what had been told them about this child; and all who heard it were amazed at what the shepherds told them. But Mary treasured all these words and pondered them in her heart. The shepherds returned, glorifying and praising God for all they had heard and seen, as it had been told them. After eight days had passed, it was time to circumcise the child; and he was called Jesus, the name given by the angel before he was conceived in the womb.

- Shepherds were not commonly regarded as ideal witnesses, given the marginal, nomadic nature of their lives. Yet we see them as among the first to announce Jesus who would proclaim himself "shepherd." I ask God to help me to receive the Gospel from unexpected sources.

- On the threshold of this new year, I prepare to receive words and memories to treasure and to ponder. I ask for God's blessing.

Thursday, 2nd January   John 1:19–28

This is the testimony given by John when the Jews sent priests and Levites from Jerusalem to ask him, "Who are you?" He confessed and did not deny it, but confessed, "I am not the Messiah." And they asked him, "What then? Are you Elijah?" He said, "I am not." "Are you the prophet?" He answered, "No." Then they said to him, "Who are you? Let us have an answer for those who sent us. What do you say about yourself?" He said, "I am the voice of one crying out in the wilderness, 'Make straight the way of the Lord,'" as the prophet Isaiah said. Now they had been sent from the Pharisees. They asked him, "Why then are you baptizing if you are neither the Messiah, nor Elijah, nor the prophet?" John answered them, "I baptize with water. Among you stands one whom you do not know, the one who is coming after me; I am not worthy to untie the thong of his sandal." This took place in Bethany across the Jordan where John was baptizing.

- In prayer God speaks words of comfort and assurance into the wildernesses of our lives—our bad moments of guilt, fears, anxieties, resentment. God speaks words that help us put ourselves into a bigger world, the world of the love of God.

- In prayer God calls each of us to be voices in the wilderness for others in their search for love, for meaning, for faith, and for God.

Friday 3rd January   John 1:29

The next day John saw Jesus coming toward him and declared, "Here is the Lamb of God who takes away the sin of the world!"

- Jesus commended John the Baptist highly. Here John shows his ability to recognize Jesus and point others to him.

- I think of how I might live more in this way.

Saturday 4th January   John 1:35–39

The next day John again was standing with two of his disciples, and as he watched Jesus walk by, he exclaimed, "Look, here is the Lamb of

God!" The two disciples heard him say this, and they followed Jesus. When Jesus turned and saw them following, he said to them, "What are you looking for?" They said to him, "Rabbi" (which translated means Teacher), "where are you staying?" He said to them, "Come and see." They came and saw where he was staying, and they remained with him that day.

- John is a signpost, drawing attention to the presence of God. He is content not to be the object of attention.

- I hear Jesus ask me, "What are you looking for?" I take time to answer with what is deep in my heart. I listen for his invitation to draw closer, "Come and see."

Sunday 5th January, The Epiphany of the Lord   Matthew 2:1–6

In the time of King Herod, after Jesus was born in Bethlehem of Judea, wise men from the East came to Jerusalem, asking, "Where is the child who has been born king of the Jews? For we observed his star at its rising, and have come to pay him homage." When King Herod heard this, he was frightened, and all Jerusalem with him; and calling together all the chief priests and scribes of the people, he inquired of them where the Messiah was to be born. They told him, "In Bethlehem of Judea; for so it has been written by the prophet: 'And you, Bethlehem, in the land of Judah, are by no means least among the rulers of Judah; for from you shall come a ruler who is to shepherd my people Israel.'"

- Herod was interested in Jesus in an intellectual way, careful that his own position not be affected. I realize that my prayer draws me into a relationship and ask that I be ready to accept the consequences that may come to light.

- The comfortable and established did not recognize Jesus, but the travellers and strangers appreciated who he was. I ask that I be open to the voices of the stranger and to wisdom from other traditions.

welcome to the advent retreat

The Advent of Jesus occurs in history, mystery, and majesty. This means that we have three Advents to consider. The First Advent is the historical coming of Jesus which occurred "long time ago, in Bethlehem," as the carol puts it. That first Advent throws light on the present time in which we live.

So we pray over the First Advent or "coming" of Jesus in history. The gospels are our starting point. Catechists prepare Nativity Plays to teach children the original nativity stories. The start of the story illuminates Christian living in the present. This is what we do all the time! Think of a family sitting down to plan for Christmas: they look back on how things went last Christmas, and that helps them shape their present plans. So too the Advent of Jesus in history illuminates our present lives as Christians: we learn how to shape our lives now by seeing how his life was shaped then.

The Second Advent is what is occurring as you read these lines. When we say that Jesus is coming "in mystery," we mean that his presence is not obvious except to the eyes of faith. Jesus comes in disguise in people and situations, in suffering and tragedy, in beauty and in joy, in the sacraments and in prayer. This coming occurs all the time. We can think of the Christian mystery as a precious diamond. It can be viewed from many aspects. It reveals its beauty no matter which way it is turned. So with the mystery of Jesus: throughout the year we view it from different aspects. We cannot take all aspects in at once, because, like the diamond, the mystery is too rich. We can say that each day is an Advent Day, but mysteriously.

Then there is the Third Advent, the future coming of Jesus in majesty. In the Creeds we say, "He will come again. . . ." This is the coming that we will focus on during this retreat: we will be asking for a glimpse of God's intended future for us.

God's coming in majesty throws light on how we are to shape things in the present. Just as the past can throw light on the present, so too the future can illuminate the present, if we know enough about it. Think of a mother preparing for the Christmas meal. She looks ahead and imagines how the meal should be. Then she decides on what items she wants to make this happen and goes off and buys what she needs. Thus the desired future shapes the present. On the negative side, weather warnings help us to prepare properly for tsunamis and hurricanes.

There is a cartoon of a man holding a placard in a chaotic world. It reads: "The end is Nigh—But I have a Plan!" If we know nothing about God's plans for us, we dread the future and fight it off. But if we take to heart the content of this retreat, we will look forward to Jesus' final Advent. "I know the plans I have for you, says the Lord, plans for your welfare and not for harm, to give you a future with hope" (Jer 29:11).

Past and future, then, are like two lighthouses, both focused on the present. Both the historical and future Advents are God's doing, not our own. God will decide, in the fullness of time, when to intervene definitively in our history. Our role is played out in the present: we play our role well when we are guided by God's past and future interventions. God respects us so much as to engage us as co-creators of the future. This means that we need to work according to divine indications. Enough of these are given us, as we shall see, to shape our present activities: we are not left floundering in the dark, and we have something precious here to offer to a confused and searching world.

Our Advent Theme: The God Who Is to Come

We want to take our direction into the New Year from the light that Jesus' future Advent offers us. Each session offers us one of Jesus' promises to reflect upon. Promises are the language of love. The promises are made to us because of the love that the Father has lavished on us (1 Jn 3:1). May you experience that love as you ponder the promises, and grow in the virtue of hope.

Your Inner Mood

God wants to meet you and tell you what wonderful things he has in store for you. Lovers do this! You will meet God in the deepest dimensions of your heart, because there you are your truest and best self. Ask then for the gift of a silent heart to be able to hear God's whisper. Then you will catch on to what God promises you this Christmastide.

This beautiful poem encourages us to listen well and to notice the ways in which God is present to us right now! Today is the only Advent day that you have in your hands:

Have you not heard his silent steps?
He comes, comes, ever comes.

Every moment and every age,
every day and every night
he comes, comes, ever comes.

Many a song have I sung
in many a mood of mind,
but all their notes have always proclaimed,
'He comes, comes, ever comes.'

In the fragrant days of sunny April
through the forest path
he comes, comes, ever comes.

In the rainy gloom of July nights
on the thundering chariot of clouds
he comes, comes, ever comes.

In sorrow after sorrow
it is his steps that press upon my heart,
and it is the golden touch of his feet
that makes my joy to shine.

—Rabindrinath Tagore

Your inner mood, then, can be one of expectancy,
alertness, and hope.

Our God

Your retreat is an inner journey, and where it may lead is as yet unknown to you. You are, however, being led by God, and as Newman says, "God knows what he's about!"

"The Lord waits to be gracious to you" (Is 30:18). God is interested only in your good. You may well be surprised or encouraged, challenged or excited at what happens. You may become puzzled or fearful: perhaps God may be hinting that your life should take a new direction—think of Our Lady at the Annunciation: her life is transformed by accepting God's proposal. May you be as receptive to the promises as Mary was: She "treasured all these words and pondered them in her heart" (Lk 2:19, 51).

By staying in prayer with an open mind and a generous heart, you will come to deep inner peace, born of being with God. Think of God as "Wonderful." Thus he is described in scripture some thirty times: he is the wonderful counselor; he does wonderful deeds. When the father of Samson asks the angel's name, the angel replies, "Why do you ask my name? It is too wonderful!" (Jgs 13:18). What then is to be said of God if even the angel is too wonderful? When we pray, we are in the presence of someone totally wonderful and gracious, so we can let our hearts respond freely.

Plan the Time

The retreat is organized into four sessions. You can complete them in a short time or spread them out over the four weeks of Advent. Go gently, at your own pace. There are advantages in going slowly: God is not in a hurry. And of course some things will attract you and leave you pondering beyond your scheduled prayer time.

Work out a set of suitable prayer times. Decide how long you are going to give yourself for each session. Rhythms help us to settle down and to anticipate what is ahead. Try to be generous: God is generous and rewards generous hearts (2 Cor 8 and 9). Half an hour may be suitable for a session. St. Ignatius suggests that whatever time you allocate to your prayer, you should be faithful to it, even if you are bored or find it difficult or distracting. Many people say "I don't feel I'm getting anywhere," but you are offering God your goodwill and your time in a busy day. You may feel useless, but God is at work, deep in your being where you cannot notice what is going on.

1. Prepare for Your Prayer Session

Attention to place, posture, and surroundings is helpful because we are people with bodies as well as minds, souls, and spirits. As the psalmist says: "Let all my being bless his holy Name" (Ps 103:1). We can tailor-make our preparations for prayer! We learn by reflecting on experience what best helps us.

So choose a suitable place where you are likely to be undisturbed: put your phone and other gadgets on silent. Create a sacred space!

Add any décor that is helpful: a flower, a seed, a candle, a picture. You may choose a piece of music, using it as a preparation or a background for your prayer.

Choose a time that suits you, and try to stay with it through the retreat, because order and rhythm and good habits help us. Decide also how long you will stay in the prayer. Prayer can be hard work sometimes. But we will not give up easily if we have promised the Lord a certain length of time for our encounter. In a Buddhist retreat you would be asked to pray for ten to fourteen hours a day! But let's not over-do it. Perhaps ten to fifteen minutes is a good length to start with.

Take up your preferred prayer posture—kneeling, sitting, or lying down. Remember that prayer is not like reading a book alone. Another person is present, though unseen. Prayer is an encounter with the mysterious Being who loves you lavishly and desires to bring you home to himself.

A breathing exercise can help you to relax and focus. One is given below. If it helps, good. If not, try another. Also provided is a meditation, with a candle as your focus. Use either exercise or others that help to focus you in attentive silence.

2. Focusing Exercises

Settle yourself. Begin to quietly breathe in and out through your nostrils. Imagine the room you are in as being filled with a coloured air. As you draw the air deep into your body through your nostrils, you can imagine this coloured air as it makes its way down from your nostrils through your throat and chest. Now, as if you had a glass body, you can see it extending from your shoulders down your arms and working its way to your fingers. See it as it travels right down to the pit of your stomach. Allow your quiet, gentle breathing pattern to bring you into a relaxed state.

Sit quietly for a few moments . . . Listen to the sounds around you . . . Take a candle in your hands . . . Feel its weight, its texture . . . Notice its colour, shape, and beauty . . . Slowly light it and place it near you . . . The candle can help you to pray . . . Watch it for a few moments, burning quietly and steadily . . . Ask to be like the candle: a quiet, steady light for the world . . . Then begin the prayer.

When you end your time of prayer, bless your candle as you extinguish it, and promise to return.

3. Begin the Prayer

Think of the phrase with which a French mystic summed up her relationship with God: "You gazed on me—and you smiled!" Allow God to smile at you, and allow yourself to smile back! Perhaps much of the prayer time is spent right here, but that will be fine! To move forward into the unknown, you need to be aware of God's infinite and unconditional love for you. St. John says, "Think of the love which the Father has given us"—but we need a stronger word than "think"! Ask to be enthused, caught up, overwhelmed by that love. You are meeting God, and God is wonderful!

Now ask for what you need. Perhaps ask Jesus, in the words of the prayer, "to see him more clearly, love him more dearly, and follow him more nearly."

Slowly read the Scripture passage that follows, as if it were a coded message that you must decipher in order to find the treasure to which it points. Perhaps instead of just reading the words, whisper them to yourself. During the rest of the day you may find yourself coming back to some phrase that has become rich and meaningful for you. The hand of God is there!

Prayer is not a spectator event, so ask God to help you to get engaged in the mystery.

4. Read the Scripture: First Promise—New Life   John 1:1–12; 10:10

To all who received him,
who believed in his name,
he gave power
to become children of God.
I came that they may have life,
and have it abundantly.

5. Imagine the Scene

I find in my imagination a comfortable place where I can be alone with Jesus. I watch expectantly at the window for him to come. I like to see him before he sees me. It gives me time to get ready. When he arrives I throw the door open in welcome. I embrace him or shake his hand, and we sit down together. We chat about ourselves for a while. Then he says, "Let's talk about my promise to make you a child of God! I'd love you to live out of that awareness for the rest of your life."

He goes on: "You're not an 'ordinary person'— you are special to me! Our friendship is changing you from the inside. You are truly a member of my family. In your heart you are becoming divine, like me, because your love is growing—you are becoming love itself. You belong more and more in divine company. People may say, 'What's happening to X?' But can you tell them that you are becoming more and more alive, because you are becoming divine? Let it be a secret between us until it is revealed fully at the End, but be convinced that it is in process now. So let your prayer be simply, 'Make me grow in love!'"

6. Reflect on Your Own Life

What happens in me as Jesus speaks? Do I laugh or cry? Does my heart feel like bursting with hope and joy? Am I full of gratitude or doubt? How do I think about myself? Do I see myself as important to God? Other questions and points of meditation include:

- Can I let the promise of Jesus into my heart? If I did, it would become the most important thing about me. It would gladden my heart and keep me going, especially in difficult times. I decide that every day I will repeat this glorious truth to myself: "I am a daughter or a son of God."

- I think of the people I meet: family, friends, passers-by on the street. I start to look at them with a new respect. I begin to see what perhaps they can't see, because no one has told them. I keep saying to myself, "That person is a son or daughter of God!" This is so enriching, that through the eyes of Jesus, I can see them as he does. I know their deepest secret!

- Everyone is transformed. Each is a glorious mystery for me. I begin to thank God for them.

Respect and reverence shine through me, and people notice the difference.

- I ask myself: Is this the way Jesus saw people? He knew their possibility, that each could become a child of God. And by his love he makes it happen. I ask Jesus that I may come to see myself as marvelous, extraordinary, and then that I may see others likewise.

- I speak with Jesus "as one friend speaks to another," to use the simple image of St. Ignatius.

7. Review the Prayer

We see things more clearly in retrospect than when they are going on. Jot down a few notes, as you might do after a dream. This will help you to reflect more deeply on what went on in the prayer. You can then ask yourself, "What went on for me?"

- What did I experience during the prayer time?
- Did I do what I could to stay focused?
- Does anything jump out that was especially appealing to me?
- Did something cause me disquiet? What might this mean?

- Might it be possible that God is asking me to change for the better in the light of his promise that I am truly his daughter or son?

- Prayer is an intimate moment in my relationship with God. So did I talk with Jesus about what matters to me? How did he talk with me? Or was I simply lost in my head, thinking, but not engaging with Jesus?

8. End the Prayer

I chat with God, with Jesus, and the Holy Spirit as my heart suggests. They are promising me that I am a family member, so I want to get to know each of them more closely. I finish with a prayer of praise:

> Glory Be to the Father, and to the Son,
> and to the Holy Spirit.
> As it was in the beginning, is now,
> and ever shall be, World without end.
> Amen.

1. Prepare for Your Prayer Session

Turn to page 64.

2. Focusing Exercises

Turn to page 65.

3. Begin the Prayer

Turn to page 66.

4. Read the Scripture: Second Promise—Comfort and Joy   John 16:20–22

"Very truly, I tell you,
you will weep and mourn,
you will have pain,
but your pain will turn into joy.
When a woman is in labour,
she has pain, because her hour has come.
But when her child is born,
she no longer remembers the anguish
because of the joy of having brought a
human being into the world.
So you have pain now;

but I will see you again,
and your hearts will rejoice,
and no one will take your joy from you."

5. Imagine the Scene

I find in my imagination a comfortable place where I can be alone with Jesus. I watch expectantly at the window for him to come. I like to see him before he sees me. It gives me time to get ready. When he arrives I throw the door open and embrace him or shake his hand, and we sit down together. We chat about ourselves for a while. Then I tell him that my heart is sore over some tragedy that has happened recently. It might be a personal issue such as a strained relationship, or a calamity like a hurricane, or the death of a friend, or the state of the Church, or whatever.

I ask him how he coped with all the suffering in his life. He is quiet for a while. Then he says, "I came to bring blessing and joy to the world, but that's hard work, and I suffered for it! But I stuck with my task because I believed that Love must win through eventually. My Father's project is great enough to cope with suffering and evil, and he works against it endlessly. Because he respects humans so much, he doesn't simply eliminate us, as in Sodom and Gomorrah or the flood when everyone bad was wiped out.

God's chosen way is to accept that evil occurs, and then to work hard to bring good out of it. That is what happened in my Passion: good came out of it, but how? Well, I tried to accept it patiently and lovingly, and that transformed it. It revealed—better than anything else I did—just how endlessly the Father and I love the human race! Our love embraced all the evil and took the sting out of it.

Even in your own life you can see good coming out of suffering! Reflect on how sickness has mellowed you: it has made you gentler and more sensitive. Look at the hidden levels of love and care that you showed in looking after your parents when they were ageing. Think of a parent who endures sleepless nights because the baby can't sleep. How spontaneous that love is, though it involves suffering! You have to do all you can to fight suffering that can be avoided; but when it's *unavoidable* and you bear it with patience and love, it brings light and love to the world. At the End, all tears will be wiped away, and you will then be filled with joy because of your endurance."

6. Reflect on Your Own Life

- What happens in me as Jesus speaks? Am I doubtful, or full of wonder? Do I thank him for transforming pain from the inside?

- I think about Jesus' Passion and I see that what he says is true. I look back over my life and notice occasions when good came from my suffering. His suffering helped the world: so can mine, if I accept it well.

- Perhaps I decide to stop grumbling when things upset me! Like Jesus, I want love to win through. I ask: "Passion of Christ, comfort me!"

- Perhaps too I feel urged to do what I can to eliminate avoidable suffering in the life of at least one person I know.

- Can I begin to look differently at the unavoidable sufferings in my life—ageing, sickness, the loss of friends—and integrate them into my relationships with God? Can I try to accept them patiently and lovingly, believing that God makes a hidden and disguised Advent to me in them?

- Jesus is saying that God's love can hold the world's pain in check. To believe in Jesus' promise would give me hope and energy.

- He talks of joy emerging from pain. Is there much joy in my life right now?

- I speak with Jesus "as one friend speaks to another," to use the simple image of St. Ignatius.

7. Review the Prayer

We see things more clearly in retrospect than when they are going on. Jot down a few notes, as you might do after a dream. This will help you to reflect more deeply on what went on in the prayer, so you can ask yourself, "What went on for me?"

- What did I experience during the prayer time?

- Did I do what I could to stay focused?

- Does anything jump out that was especially appealing to me?

- Did something cause me disquiet? What might this mean?

- Might it be possible that God is asking me to change my attitudes to suffering and pain?

- Prayer is an intimate moment in my relationship with God. So did I talk with Jesus about what matters to me? How did he talk with me? Or was I simply lost in my head, thinking, but not engaging with Jesus?

8. End the Prayer

I chat with God, with Jesus, and the Holy Spirit as my heart suggests. I am a family member of theirs, so I want to be in tune with the ways in which they face suffering and evil. The first two promises are connected!

I finish with a prayer of praise: Glory Be . . .

session three

1. Prepare for Your Prayer Session

Turn to page 64.

2. Focusing Exercises

Turn to page 65.

3. Begin the Prayer

Turn to page 66.

4. Read the Scripture: Third Promise—Resurrection   John 11:25–26

"I am the resurrection and the life.
Those who believe in me,
even though they die,
will live,
and everyone who lives and believes in me
will never die.
Do you believe this?"

5. Imagine the Scene

I find in my imagination a comfortable place where I can be alone with Jesus. I watch expectantly at the window for him to come. I like to see him before he sees me. It gives me time to get ready. When he arrives I throw the door open and embrace him or shake his hand, and we sit down together. We chat about ourselves for a while. Then I begin to speak with him about a bereavement I have had, and the pain of loss I experience.

I imagine him responding somewhat as follows: "My Father could have eliminated death for everyone when he raised me from the dead. But for his own wise reasons he didn't. Instead he decided to make human death a transforming moment; it is no longer 'the end,' like a blank wall. Instead it is the passageway for entry into the fullness of divine life. My promise to you is that real life—the best life—gets under way after you die. Death hollows you out so that you can be overwhelmed by the life and love that God has for you. This life is a preparation for something infinitely better than you can now imagine. Do you believe this?"

6. Reflect on Your Own Life

- What happens in me as Jesus speaks? Does my heart feel like bursting with hope and joy, or am I doubtful?

- What do I say to Jesus' question? Do I believe in my own resurrection or do I not? I ask for faith and hope in this promise.

- Do I believe that in fact there are no "dead people"—only persons who have moved through death into limitless life?

- What do I now think of all the friends I have loved? Have I really "lost them" in their dying or are they awaiting me in hope?

- To believe in Jesus' promise would open out my life. It would also transform how I see others— especially those I don't like! They will be my eternal companions.

- I speak with Jesus "as one friend speaks to another," to use the simple image of St. Ignatius.

7. Review the Prayer

We see things more clearly in retrospect than when they are going on. Jot down a few notes, as you might do after a dream. This will help you to reflect more deeply on what went on in the prayer, so you can ask yourself, "What went on for me?"

- What did I experience during the prayer time?

- Did I do what I could to stay focused?

- Does anything jump out that was especially appealing to me?

- Did something cause me disquiet? What might this mean?

- Might it be possible that God is asking me to change my attitudes to suffering and pain?

- Prayer is an intimate moment in my relationship with God. So did I talk with Jesus about what matters to me? How did he talk with me? Or was I simply lost in my head, thinking, but not engaging with Jesus?

8. End the Prayer

I chat with God, with Jesus, and the Holy Spirit as my heart suggests. I am already a family member of theirs. The mystery I carry is that I am becoming divine, and that this process goes on even in the suffering and pain I endure. It will be brought to full flower in my resurrection!

I finish with a prayer of praise: Glory Be . . .

session four

1. Prepare for Your Prayer Session

Turn to page 64.

2. Focusing Exercises

Turn to page 65.

3. Begin the Prayer

Turn to page 66.

4. Read the Scripture: Fourth Promise—Eternal Celebration   John 14:1–3

"Do not let your hearts be troubled.
Believe in God, believe also in me.
In my Father's house
there are many dwelling-places.
If it were not so,
would I have told you
that I go to prepare a place for you?
And if I go and prepare a place for you,
I will come again
and will take you to myself,
so that where I am,
there you may be also."

5. Imagine the Scene

I find in my imagination a comfortable place where I can be alone with Jesus. I watch expectantly at the window for him to come. I like to see him before he sees me. It gives me time to get ready. When he arrives I throw the door open and embrace him or shake his hand, and we sit down together. We chat about ourselves for a while. Then I ask him yet another question about the future. He has already hinted at what my new life with him is like. Further, he has sketched out how God weaves my pain and suffering into the divine project for the world; and he has promised me the unparalleled gift of resurrection. Now I ask him, "What will it be like when we are all gathered in, and forever?" Perhaps he smiles and says: "Imagine this world free from wars, want, hate, greed, and all forms of domination. Imagine that everyone is reconciled, that good relationships prevail everywhere. All of us are 'for' one another. Picture everyone at their best, all divinized. Think of transfigured humankind as one body, full of joy, love and creativity. The glory that is our destiny will shine out. Imagine God, who loves each of us specially, orchestrating the festival of the redeemed.

The surprise party for the prodigal son—the robe, ring, sandals, fatted calf, celebration, music, dancing—gives a tiny hint of the final ever-flowing celebration which we call 'heaven.' But it's not just a distant promise: wherever people foster or restore good relationships and are 'for' each other, you have it in the making, right under your eyes. Of course it's fragile and hidden now, whereas then it will be enduring and fully revealed."

6. Reflect on Your Own Life

- What happens in me as Jesus speaks? Do I laugh or cry? Does my heart feel like bursting with hope and joy, or am I doubtful, or silent with wonder and hope?

- Perhaps I feel an energy inside me to put more time and effort into building good and healthy relationships around me. If I do, surely I will notice a quiet joy in my heart—no matter what the outcome. Nothing done in love is ever wasted.

- When I take all Jesus' promises together, I find changes going on in my heart. Life takes on new colour and meaning. People, including myself, are no longer dull, uninteresting, predictable. Life is no longer boring: it's a great drama! Suffering and death are not the end; they are moments out of which God creatively brings new life.

- I speak with Jesus "as one friend speaks to another," to use St. Ignatius's simple phrase.

7. Review the Prayer

We see things more clearly in retrospect than when they are going on. Jot down a few notes, as you might do after a dream. This will help you to reflect more deeply on what went on in the prayer. You can ask yourself, "What went on for me?"

- What did I experience during the prayer time?

- Did I do what I could to stay focused?

- Does anything jump out that was especially appealing to me?

- Did something cause me disquiet? What might this mean?

- Is God inviting me to live out my life in the light of his dramatic promises?

- Prayer is an intimate moment in my relationship with God. So did I talk with Jesus about what matters to me? How did he talk with me? Or was I simply lost in my head, thinking, but not engaging with Jesus?

8. End the Prayer

I chat with God, with Jesus, and the Holy Spirit as my heart suggests. They have set up my life for joy and glory; their promises are intended to keep me going in dark times. They need my help *now* to move their project forward in our tired and confused world. When I say, "Speak, Lord, your servant is listening," do I hear them whispering something to me?

I finish with a prayer of praise: Glory Be . . .

conclusion

Review the Retreat

Take a little time to look back over this Advent retreat. Living in a world of consumerism, we run the risk of becoming consumers of grace. Grace is not "cheap." And so you might ask Jesus that the grace of this retreat may not be lost in the bustle of life. It can help to write down what you want to carry away with you so you don't forget.

You might ask:

- What did I want from the retreat? Was it given to me?

- What word of God touched me most?

- Did I experience the Lord gazing on me, and smiling?

- Where did I experience challenge, or difficulty and resistance?

- Were there moments of light, moments of darkness?

- Did I feel a deepening of a good desire, or an inspiration?

- Have I become a bit more like Jesus? He has been showing me the depth of his love. As his friend, I am to show in my time and place the depth of that love.

The Father, Son, and Spirit have been my faithful companions throughout the retreat, so I end by praising them for what they have done in me:

> Glory to you, Source of all Being
> Eternal Word
> and Holy Spirit.
> As it was in the beginning,
> Is now
> And ever shall be,
> World without end.
> Amen!

Founded in 1865, Ave Maria Press,
a ministry of the Congregation of
Holy Cross, is a Catholic publishing
company that serves the spiritual and
formative needs of the Church and its
schools, institutions, and ministers;
Christian individuals and families; and
others seeking spiritual nourishment.

———————

For a complete listing of titles from

Ave Maria Press

Sorin Books

Forest of Peace

Christian Classics

visit www.avemariapress.com

ave maria press® / Notre Dame, IN 46556
A Ministry of the United States Province of Holy Cross